# Judaism

## By
## Israel Abrahams

# JUDAISM

## CHAPTER I

### THE LEGACY FROM THE PAST

The aim of this little book is to present in brief outline some of the leading conceptions of the religion familiar since the Christian Era under the name Judaism.

The word 'Judaism' occurs for the first time at about 100 B.C., in the Graeco-Jewish literature. In the second book of the Maccabees (ii. 21, viii. 1), 'Judaism' signifies the religion of the Jews as contrasted with Hellenism, the religion of the Greeks. In the New Testament (Gal. i. 13) the same word seems to denote the Pharisaic system as an antithesis to the Gentile Christianity. In Hebrew the corresponding noun never occurs in the Bible, and it is rare even in the Rabbinic books. When it does meet us, Jahaduth implies the monotheism of the Jews as opposed to the polytheism of the heathen.

Thus the term 'Judaism' did not pass through quite the same transitions as did the name 'Jew.' Judaism appears from the first as a religion transcending tribal bounds. The 'Jew,' on the other hand, was originally a Judaean, a member of the Southern Confederacy called in the Bible Judah, and by the Greeks and Romans Judaea. Soon, however, 'Jew' came to include what had earlier been the Northern Confederacy of Israel as well, so that in the post-exilic period Jehudi or 'Jew' means an adherent of Judaism without regard to local nationality.

Judaism, then, is here taken to represent that later development of the Religion of Israel which began with the reorganisation after the Babylonian Exile (444 B.C.), and was crystallised by the Roman Exile (during the first centuries of the Christian Era). The exact period which will be here seized as a starting-point is the moment when the people of Israel were losing, never so far to regain, their territorial association with Palestine, and were becoming (what they have ever since been) a community as distinct from a nation. They remained, it is true, a distinct race, and this is still in a sense true. Yet at various periods a number of proselytes have been admitted, and in other ways the purity of the race has been affected. At all events territorial nationality ceased from a date which may be roughly fixed at 135 A.D., when the last desperate revolt under Bar-Cochba failed, and Hadrian drew his Roman plough over the city of Jerusalem and the

Temple area. A new city with a new name arose on the ruins. The ruins afterwards reasserted themselves, and Aelia Capitolina as a designation of Jerusalem is familiar only to archaeologists.

But though the name of Hadrian's new city has faded, the effect of its foundation remained. Aelia Capitolina, with its market-places and theatre, replaced the olden narrow-streeted town; a House of Venus reared its stately form in the north, and a Sanctuary to Jupiter covered, in the east, the site of the former Temple. Heathen colonists were introduced, and the Jew, who was to become in future centuries an alien everywhere, was made by Hadrian an alien in his fatherland. For the Roman Emperor denied to Jews the right of entry into Jerusalem. Thus Hadrian completed the work of Titus, and Judaism was divorced from its local habitation. More unreservedly than during the Babylonian Exile, Judaism in the Roman Exile perforce became the religion of a community and not of a state; and Israel for the first time constituted a Church. But it was a Church with no visible home. Christianity for several centuries was to have a centre at Rome, Islam at Mecca. But Judaism had and has no centre at all.

It will be obvious that the aim of the present book makes it both superfluous and inappropriate to discuss the vexed problems connected with the origins of the Religion of Israel, its aspects in primitive times, its passage through a national to an ethical monotheism, its expansion into the universalism of the second Isaiah. What concerns us here is merely the legacy which the Religion of Israel bequeathed to Judaism as we have defined it. This legacy and the manner in which it was treasured, enlarged, and administered will occupy us in the rest of this book.

But this much must be premised. If the Religion of Israel passed through the stages of totemism, animism, and polydemonism; if it was indebted to Canaanite, Kenite, Babylonian, Persian, Greek, and other foreign influences; if it experienced a stage of monolatry or henotheism (in which Israel recognised one God, but did not think of that God as the only God of all men) before ethical monotheism of the universalistic type was reached; if, further, all these stages and the moral and religious ideas connected with each left a more or less clear mark in the sacred literature of Israel; then the legacy which Judaism received from its past was a syncretism of the whole of the religious experiences of Israel as interpreted in the light of Israel's latest, highest, most approved standards. Like the Bourbon, the Jew forgets nothing; but unlike the Bourbon, the Jew is always learning. The domestic stories of the Patriarchs were not rejected as unprofitable when Israel became deeply impregnated with the monogamous teachings of writers like the author of the last chapter of Proverbs; the character of David was idealised by the spiritual associations of the Psalter, parts of which tradition ascribed to him; the earthly life was etherialised and much of the sacred literature reinterpreted in the light of an added belief in immortality; God, in the early literature a tribal non-moral deity, was in the later literature a righteous ruler who with Amos and Hosea loved and demanded righteousness in man. Judaism took over as one indivisible body of sacred teachings both the early and the later literature in which these varying conceptions of God were enshrined; the Law was accepted as the guiding rule of life, the ritual of ceremony and sacrifice was treasured as a holy memory, and as a memory not contradictory of the prophetic exaltation of inward religion but as consistent with that exaltation, as interpreting it, as but another aspect of Micah's enunciation of the demands of God: 'What doth the Lord require of thee but to do justly, to love mercy, and to walk humbly with thy God?'

Judaism, in short, included for the Jew all that had gone before. But for St. Paul's attitude of hostility to the Law, but for the deep-seated conviction that the Pauline Christianity was a denial of the Jewish monotheism, the Jew might have accepted much of the teaching of Jesus as an integral part of Judaism. In the realm of ideas which he conceived as belonging to his tradition the Jew was not logical; he did not pick and choose; he absorbed the whole. In the Jewish theology of all ages we find the most obvious contradictions. There was no attempt at reconciliation of such contradictions; they were juxtaposed in a mechanical mixture, there was no chemical compound. The Jew was always a man of moods, and his religion responded to those varying phases of feeling and belief and action. Hence such varying judgments have been formed of him and his religion. If, after the mediaeval philosophy had attempted to systematise Judaism, the religion remained unsystematic, it is easy to understand that in the earlier centuries of the Christian Era contradictions between past and present, between different strata of religious thought, caused no trouble to the Jew so long as those contradictions could be fitted into his general scheme of life. Though he was the product of development, development was an idea foreign to his conception of the ways of God with man. And to this extent he was right. For though men's ideas of God change, God Himself is changeless. The Jew transferred the changelessness of God to men's changing ideas about him. With childlike naivete he accepted all, he adopted all, and he syncretised it all as best he could into the loose system on which Pharisaism grafted itself. The legacy of the past thus was the past.

One element in the legacy was negative. The Temple and the Sacrificial system were gone for ever. That this must have powerfully affected Judaism goes without saying. Synagogue replaced Temple, prayer assumed the function of sacrifice, penitence and not the blood of bulls supplied the ritual of atonement. Events had prepared the way for this change and had prevented it attaining the character of an upheaval. For synagogues had grown up all over the land soon after the fifth century B.C.; regular services of prayer with instruction in the Scriptures had been established long before the Christian Era; the inward atonement had been preferred to, or at least associated with, the outward rite before the outward rite was torn away. It may be that, as Professor Burkitt has suggested, the awful experiences of the fall of Jerusalem and the destruction of the Temple produced within Pharisaism a moral reformation which drove the Jew within and thus spiritualised Judaism. For undoubtedly the Pharisee of the Gospels is by no means the Pharisee as we meet him in the Jewish books. There was always a latent power and tendency in Judaism towards inward religion; and it may be that this power was intensified, this tendency encouraged, by the loss of Temple and its Sacrificial rites.

But though the Temple had gone the Covenant remained. Not so much in name as in essence. We do not hear much of the Covenant in the Rabbinic books, but its spirit pervades Judaism. Of all the legacy of the past the Covenant was the most inspiring element. Beginning with Abraham, the Covenant established a special relation between God and Abraham's seed. 'I have known him, that he may command his children and his household after him, that they may keep the way of the Lord to do righteousness and judgment' (Gen. xviii. 19). Of this Covenant, the outward sign was the rite of circumcision. Renewed with Moses, and followed in traditional opinion by the Ten Commandments, the Sinaitic Covenant was a further link in the bond between God and His people. Of this Mosaic Covenant the outward sign was the Sabbath. It is of no moment for our present argument whether Abraham and Moses were historical persons or figments of tradition. A Gamaliel would have as little doubted their reality as would a St. Paul. And whatever Criticism may be doing with Abraham, it is coming more and more to see that behind the eighth-century prophets there must have towered the figure of a, if not of the traditional, Moses; behind the prophets a, if not the, Law. Be that as it may, to the Jew of the Christian Era, Abraham and Moses were real and the Covenant unalterable. By the syncretism which has been already described Jeremiah's New Covenant was not regarded as new. Nor was it new; it represented a change of stress, not of contents. When he said (Jer. xxxi. 33), 'This is the covenant which I will make with the house of Israel, after those days, saith the Lord; I will put my law in their inward parts, and in their heart will I write it,' Jeremiah, it has been held, was making Christianity possible. But he was also making Judaism possible. Here and nowhere else is to be found the principle which enabled Judaism to survive the loss of Temple and nationality. And the New Covenant was in no sense inconsistent with the Old. For not only does Jeremiah proceed to add in the self-same verse, 'I will be their God, and they will be my people,' but the New Covenant is specifically made with the house of Judah and of Israel, and it is associated with the permanence of the seed of Israel as a separate people and with the Divine rebuilding of Jerusalem. The Jew had no thought of analysing these verses into the words of the true Jeremiah and those of his editors. The point is that over and above, in complementary explanation of, the Abrahamic and Mosaic Covenants with their external signs, over and above the Call of the Patriarch and the Theophany of Sinai, was the Jeremian Covenant written in Israel's heart.

The Covenant conferred a distinction and imposed a duty. It was a bond between a gracious God and a grateful Israel. It dignified history, for it interpreted history in terms of providence and purpose; it transfigured virtue by making virtue service; it was the salt of life, for how could present degradation demoralise, seeing that God was in it, to fulfil His part of the bond, to hold Israel as His jewel, though Rome might despise? The Covenant made the Jew self-confident and arrogant, but these very faults were needed to save him. It was his only defence against the world's scorn. He forgot that the correlative of the Covenant was Isaiah's 'Covenant-People'—missionary to the Gentiles and the World. He relegated his world-mission (which Christianity and Islam in part gloriously fulfilled) to a dim Messianic future, and was content if in his own present he remained faithful to his mission to himself.

Above all, the legacy from the past came to Judaism hallowed and humanised by all the experience of redemption and suffering which had marked Israel's course in ages past, and was to mark his course in ages to come. The Exodus, the Exile, the Maccabean heroism, the Roman catastrophe; Prophet, Wise Man, Priest and Scribe,—all had left their trace. Judaism was a religion based on a book and on a tradition; but it was also a religion based on a unique experience. The book might be misread, the tradition encumbered, but the experience was eternally clear and inspiring. It shone through the Roman Diaspora as it afterwards illuminated the Roman Ghetto, making the present tolerable by the memory of the past and the hope of the future.

# CHAPTER II

# RELIGION AS LAW

The feature of Judaism which first attracts an outsider's attention, and which claims a front place in this survey, is its 'Nomism' or 'Legalism.' Life was placed under the control of Law. Not only morality, but religion also, was codified. 'Nomism,' it has been truly said, 'has always formed a fundamental trait of Judaism, one of whose chief aims has ever been to mould life in all its varying relations according to the Law, and to make obedience to the commandments a necessity and a custom' (Lauterbach, Jewish Encyclopedia, ix. 326). Only the latest development of Judaism is away from this direction. Individualism is nowadays replacing the olden solidarity. Thus, at the Central Conference of American Rabbis, held in July 1906 at Indianapolis, a project to formulate a system of laws for modern use was promptly rejected. The chief modern problem in Jewish life is just this: To what extent, and in what manner, can Judaism still place itself under the reign of Law?

But for many centuries, certainly up to the French Revolution, Religion as Law was the dominant conception in Judaism. Before examining the validity of this conception a word is necessary as to the mode in which it expressed itself. Conduct, social and individual, moral and ritual, was regulated in the minutest details. As the Dayan M. Hyamson has said, the maxim De minimis non curat lex was not applicable to the Jewish Law. This Law was a system of opinion and of practice and of feeling in which the great principles of morality, the deepest concerns of spiritual religion, the genuinely essential requirements of ritual, all found a prominent place. To assert that Pharisaism included the small and excluded the great, that it enforced rules and forgot principles, that it exalted the letter and neglected the spirit, is a palpable libel. Pharisaism was founded on God. On this foundation was erected a structure which embraced the eternal principles of religion. But the system, it must be added, went far beyond this. It held that there was a right and a wrong way of doing things in themselves trivial. Prescription ruled in a stupendous array of matters which other systems deliberately left to the fancy, the judgment, the conscience of the individual. Law seized upon the whole life, both in its inward experiences and outward manifestations. Harnack characterises the system harshly enough. Christianity did not add to Judaism, it subtracted. Expanding a famous epigram of Wellhausen's, Harnack admits that everything taught in the Gospels 'was also to be found in the Prophets, and even in the Jewish tradition of their time. The Pharisees themselves were in possession of it; but, unfortunately, they were in possession of much else besides. With them it was weighted, darkened, distorted, rendered ineffective and deprived of its force by a thousand things which they also held to be religious, and every whit as important as mercy and judgment. They reduced everything into one fabric; the good and holy was only one woof in a broad earthly warp' (What is Christianity? p. 47). It is necessary to qualify this judgment, but it does bring out the all-pervadingness of Law in Judaism. 'And thou shalt speak of them when thou sittest in thine house, when thou walkest by the way, when thou liest down and when thou risest up' (Deut. vi. 7). The Word of God was to occupy the Jew's thoughts constantly; in his daily employment and during his manifold activities; when at work and when at rest. And as a correlative, the Law must direct this complex life, the Code must authorise action or forbid it, must turn the thoughts and emotions in one direction and divert them from another.

Nothing in the history of religions can be cited as a complete parallel to this. But incomplete parallels abound. A very large portion of all men's lives is regulated from without: by the Bible and other sacred books; by the institutions and rites of religion; by the law of the land; by the imposed rules of accepted guides, poets, philosophers, physicians; and above all by social conventions, current fashions, and popular maxims. Only in the rarest case is an exceptional man the monstrosity which, we are told, every Israelite was in the epoch of the Judges—a law unto himself.

But in Judaism, until the period of modern reform, this fact of human life was not merely an unconscious truism, it was consciously admitted. And it was realised in a Code.

Or rather in a series of Codes. First came the Mishnah, a Code compiled at about the year 200 A.D., but the result of a Pharisaic activity extending over more than two centuries. While Christianity was producing the Gospels and the rest of the New Testament—the work in large part of Jews, or of men born in the circle of Judaism—Judaism in its other manifestation was working at the Code known as the Mishnah. This word means 'repetition,' or 'teaching by repetition'; it was an oral tradition reduced to writing long after much of its contents had been sifted in the discussions of the schools. In part earlier and in part later than the Mishnah was the Midrash ('inquiry,' 'interpretation'), not a Code, but a two-fold exposition of Scripture; homiletic with copious use of parable, and legalistic with an eye to the regulation of conduct. Then came the Talmud in two recensions, the Palestinian and the Babylonian, the latter completed about 500 A.D. For some centuries afterwards the Geonim (heads of the Rabbinical Universities in Persia) continued to analyse and define the legal prescriptions and ritual of Judaism, adding and changing in accord with the needs of the day; for Tradition was a living, fluid thing. Then in the eleventh century Isaac of Fez (Alfasi) formulated a guide to Talmudic Law, and about a hundred years later (1180) Maimonides produced his Strong Hand, a Code of law and custom which influenced Jewish life ever after. Other codifications were made; but finally, in the sixteenth century, Joseph Caro (mystic and legalist) compiled the Table Prepared (Shulchan Aruch), which, with masterly skill, collected the whole of the traditional law, arranged it under convenient heads in chapters and paragraphs, and carried down to our own day the Rabbinic conception of life. Under this Code, with more or less relaxation, the great bulk of Jews still live. But the revolt against it, or emancipation from it, is progressing every year, for the olden Jewish conception of religion and the old Jewish theory of life are, as hinted above, becoming seriously undermined.

Now in what precedes there has been some intentional ambiguity in the use of the word Law. Much of the misunderstanding of Judaism has arisen from this ambiguity. 'Law' is in no adequate sense what the Jews themselves understood by the nomism of their religion. In modern times Law and Religion tend more and more to separate, and to speak of Judaism as Law eo ipso implies a divorce of Judaism from Religion. The old antithesis between letter and spirit is but a phase of the same criticism. Law must specify, and the lawyer interprets Acts of Parliament by their letter; he refuses to be guided by the motives of the Act, he is concerned with what the Act distinctly formulates in set terms. In this sense Judaism never was a Legal Religion. It did most assiduously seek to get to the underlying motives of the written laws, and all the expansions of the Law were based on a desire more fully to realise the meaning and intention of the written Code. In other words, the Law was looked upon as the expression of the Will of God. Man was to yield to that Will for two reasons. First, because God is the perfect ideal of goodness. That ideal was for man to revere, and, so far as in him lay, to imitate. 'As I am merciful, be thou merciful; because I am gracious, be thou gracious.' The 'Imitation of God' is a notion which constantly meets us in Rabbinic literature. It is based on the Scriptural text: 'Be ye holy, for I the Lord am holy.' 'God, the ideal of all morality, is the founder of man's moral nature.' This is Professor Lazarus' modern way of putting it. But in substance it is the Jewish conception through all the ages. And there is a second reason. The Jew would not have understood the possibility of any other expression of the Divine Will than the expression which Judaism enshrined. For though he held that the Law was something imposed from without, he identified this imposed Law with the law which his own moral nature posited. The Rabbis tell us that certain things in the written Law could have been reached by man without the Law. The Law was in large part a correspondence to man's moral nature. This Rabbinic idea Lazarus sums up in the epigram: 'Moral laws, then, are not laws because they are written; they are written because they are laws.' The moral principle is autonomous, but its archetype is God. The ultimate reason, like the highest aim of morality, should be in itself. The threat of punishment and the promise of reward are the psychologic means to secure the fulfilment of laws, never the reasons for the laws, nor the motives to action. It is easy and necessary sometimes to praise and justify eudemonism, but, as Lazarus adds, 'Not a state to be reached, not a good to be won, not an evil to be warded off, is the impelling force of morality, but itself furnishes the creative impulse, the supreme commanding authority' (Ethics of Judaism, I. chap, ii.). And so the Rabbi of the third century B.C., Antigonos of Socho, put it in the memorable saying: 'Be not like servants who minister to their master upon the condition of receiving a reward; but be like servants who minister to their master without the condition of receiving a reward; and let the Fear of heaven be upon you' (Aboth, i. 3).

Clearly the multiplication of rules obscures principles. The object of codification, to get at the full meaning of principles, is defeated by its own success. For it is always easier to follow rules than to apply principles. Virtues are more attainable than virtue, characteristics than character. And while it is false to assert that Judaism attached more importance to ritual than to religion, yet, the two being placed on one and the same plane, it is possible to find in co-existence ritual piety and moral baseness. Such a combination is ugly, and people do not stop to think whether the baseness would be more or less if the ritual piety were absent instead of present. But it is the fact that on the whole the Jewish codification of religion did not produce the evil results possible or even likely to accrue. The Jew was always distinguished for his domestic virtues, his purity of life, his sobriety, his charity, his devotion. These were the immediate consequence of his Law-abiding disposition and theory. Perhaps there was some lack of enthusiasm, something too much of the temperate. But the facts of life always brought their corrective. Martyrdom was the means by which the Jewish consciousness was kept at a glowing heat. And as the Jew was constantly called upon to die for his religion, the religion ennobled the life which was willingly surrendered for the religion. The Messianic Hope was vitalised by persecution. The Jew, devotee of practical ideals, became also a dreamer. His visions of God were ever present to remind him that the law which he codified was to him the Law of God.

# CHAPTER III

## ARTICLES OF FAITH

It is often said that Judaism left belief free while it put conduct into fetters. Neither half of this assertion is strictly true. Belief was not free altogether; conduct was not altogether controlled. In the Mishnah (Sanhedrin, x. 1) certain classes of unbelievers are pronounced portionless in the world to come. Among those excluded from Paradise are men who deny the resurrection of the dead, and men who refuse assent to the doctrine of the Divine origin of the Torah, or Scripture. Thus it cannot be said that belief was, in the Rabbinic system, perfectly free. Equally inaccurate is the assertion that conduct was entirely a matter of prescription. Not only were men praised for works of supererogation, performance of more than the Law required; not only were there important divergences in the practical rules of conduct formulated by the various Rabbis; but there was a whole class of actions described as 'matters given over to the heart,' delicate refinements of conduct which the law left untouched and were a concern exclusively of the feeling, the private judgment of the individual. The right of private judgment was passionately insisted on in matters of conduct, as when Rabbi Joshua refused to be guided as to his practical decisions by the Daughter of the Voice, the supernatural utterance from on high. The Law, he contended, is on earth, not in heaven; and man must be his own judge in applying the Law to his own life and time. And, the Talmud adds, God Himself announced that Rabbi Joshua was right.

Thus there was neither complete fluidity of doctrine nor complete rigidity of conduct. There was freedom of conduct within the law, and there was law within freedom of doctrine.

But Dr. Emil Hirsch puts the case fairly when he says: 'In the same sense as Christianity or Islam, Judaism cannot be credited with Articles of Faith. Many attempts have indeed been made at systematising and reducing to a fixed phraseology and sequence the contents of the Jewish religion. But these have always lacked the one essential element: authoritative sanction on the part of a supreme ecclesiastical body' (Jewish Encyclopedia, ii. 148).

Since the epoch of the Great Sanhedrin, there has been no central authority recognised throughout Jewry. The Jewish organisation has long been congregational. Since the fourth century there has been no body with any jurisdiction over the mass of Jews. At that date the Calendar was fixed by astronomical calculations. The Patriarch, in Babylon, thereby voluntarily abandoned the hold he had previously had over the scattered Jews, for it was no longer the fiat of the Patriarch that settled the dates of the Festivals. While there was something like a central authority, the Canon of Scripture had been fixed by Synods, but there is no record of any attempt to promulgate articles of faith. During the revolt against Hadrian an Assembly of Rabbis was held at Lydda. It was then decided that a Jew must yield his life rather than accept safety from the Roman power, if such conformity involved one of the three offences: idolatry, murder, and unchastity (including, incest and adultery). But while this decision throws a favourable light on the Rabbinic theory of life, it can in no sense be called a fixation of a creed. There were numerous synods in the Middle Ages, but they invariably dealt with practical morals or with the problems which arose from time to time in regard to the relations between Jews and their Christian neighbours. It is true that we occasionally read of excommunications for heresy. But in the case, for instance, of Spinoza, the Amsterdam Synagogue was much more anxious to dissociate itself from the heresies of Spinoza than to compel Spinoza to conform to the beliefs of the Synagogue. And though this power of excommunication might have been employed by the mediaeval Rabbis to enforce the acceptance of a creed, in point of fact no such step was ever taken.

Since the time of Moses Mendelssohn (1728-1786), the chief Jewish dogma has been that Judaism has no dogmas. In the sense assigned above this is clearly true. Dogmas imposed by an authority able and willing to enforce conformity and punish dissent are non-existent in Judaism. In olden times membership of the religion of Judaism was almost entirely a question of birth and race, not of confession. Proselytes were admitted by circumcision and baptism, and nothing beyond an acceptance of the Unity of God and the abjuration of idolatry is even now required by way of profession from a proselyte. At the same time the earliest passage put into the public liturgy was the Shema' (Deuteronomy vi. 4-9), in which the unity of God and the duty to love God are expressed. The Ten Commandments were also recited daily in the Temple. It is instructive to note the reason given for the subsequent removal of the Decalogue from the daily liturgy. It was feared that some might assume that the Decalogue comprised the whole of the binding law. Hence the prominent position given to them in the Temple service was no longer assigned to the Ten Commandments in the ritual of the Synagogue. In modern times, however, there is a growing practice of reading the Decalogue every Sabbath day.

What we do find in Pharisaic Judaism, and this is the real answer to Harnack (supra, p. 15), is an attempt to reduce the whole Law to certain fundamental principles. When a would-be proselyte accosted Hillel, in the reign of Herod, with the demand that the Rabbi should communicate the whole of Judaism while the questioner stood on one foot, Hillel made the famous reply: 'What thou hatest do unto no man; that is the whole Law, the rest is commentary.' This recalls another famous summarisation, that given by Jesus later on in the Gospel. A little more than a century later, Akiba said that the command to love one's neighbour is the fundamental principle of the Law. Ben Azzai chose for this distinction another sentence: 'This is the book of the generations of man,' implying the equality of all men in regard to the love borne by God for His creatures. Another Rabbi, Simlai (third century), has this remarkable saying: 'Six hundred and thirteen precepts were imparted unto Moses, three hundred and sixty-five negative (in correspondence with the days of the solar year), and two hundred and forty-eight positive (in correspondence with the number of a man's limbs). David came and established them as eleven, as it is written: A psalm of David—Lord who shall sojourn in Thy tent, who shall dwell in Thy holy mountain? (i) He that walketh uprightly and (ii) worketh righteousness and (iii) speaketh the truth in his heart. (iv) He that backbiteth not with his tongue, (v) nor doeth evil to his neighbour, (vi) nor taketh up a reproach against another; (vii) in whose eyes a reprobate is despised, (viii) but who honoureth them that fear the Lord. (ix) He that sweareth to his own hurt, and changeth not; (x) He that putteth not out his money to usury, (xi) nor taketh a bribe against the innocent. He that doeth these things shall never be moved. Thus David reduced the Law to eleven principles. Then came Micah and reduced them to three, as it is written: 'What doth the Lord require of thee but (i) to do justice, (ii) to love mercy, and (iii) to walk humbly with thy God? Then came Habbakuk and made the whole Law stand on one fundamental idea, 'The righteous man liveth by his faith' (Makkoth, 23 b).

This desire to find one or a few general fundamental passages on which the whole Scripture might be seen to base itself is, however, far removed from anything of the nature of the Christian Creeds or of the Mohammedan Kalimah. And when we remember that the Pharisees and Sadducees differed on questions of doctrine (such as the belief in immortality held by the former and rejected by the latter), it becomes clear that the absence of a formal declaration of faith must have been deliberate. The most that was done was to introduce into the Liturgy a paragraph in which the assembled worshippers declared their assent to the truth and permanent validity of the Word of God. After the Shema' (whose contents are summarised above), the assembled worshippers daily recited a passage in which they said (and still say): 'True and firm is this Thy word unto us for ever.... True is it that Thou art indeed our God ... and there is none beside Thee.'

After all, the difference between Pharisee and Sadducee was political rather than theological. It was not till Judaism came into contact, contact alike of attraction and repulsion, with other systems that a desire or a need for formulating Articles of Faith was felt. Philo, coming under the Hellenic spirit, was thus the first to make the attempt. In the last chapter of the tract on the Creation (De Opifico, lxi.), Philo enumerates what he terms the five most beautiful lessons, superior to all others. These are—(i) God is; (ii) God is One; (iii) the World was created (and is not eternal); (iv) the World is one, like unto God in singleness; and (v) God exercises a continual providence for the benefit of the world, caring for His creatures like a parent for his children.

Philo's lead found no imitators. It was not for many centuries that two causes led the Synagogue to formulate a creed. And even then it was not the Synagogue as a body that acted, nor was it a creed that resulted. The first cause was the rise of sects within the Synagogue. Of these sects the most important was that of the Karaites or Scripturalists. Rejecting tradition, the Karaites expounded their beliefs both as a justification of themselves against the Traditionalists and possibly as a remedy against their own tendency to divide within their own order into smaller sects. In the middle of the twelfth century the Karaite Judah Hadassi of Constantinople arranged the whole Pentateuch under the headings of the Decalogue, much as Philo had done long before. And so he formulates ten dogmas of Judaism. These are—(i) Creation (as opposed to the Aristotelian doctrine of the eternity of the world); (ii) the existence of God; (iii) God is one and incorporeal; (iv) Moses and the other canonical prophets were called by God; (v) the Law is the Word of God, it is complete, and the Oral Tradition was unnecessary; (vi) the Law must be read by the Jew in the original Hebrew; (vii) the Temple of Jerusalem was the place chosen by God for His manifestation; (viii) the Resurrection of the dead; (ix) the Coming of Messiah, son of David; (x) Final Judgment and Retribution.

Within the main body of the Synagogue we have to wait for the same moment for a formulation of Articles of Faith. Maimonides (1135-1204) was a younger contemporary of Hadassi; he it was that drew up the one and only set of principles which have ever enjoyed wide authority in Judaism. Before Maimonides there had been some inclination towards a creed, but he is the first to put one into set terms. Maimonides was much influenced by

Aristotelianism, and this gave him an impulse towards a logical statement of the tenets of Judaism. On the other side, he was deeply concerned by the criticism of Judaism from the side of Mohammedan theologians. The latter contended, in particular, that the biblical anthropomorphisms were destructive of a belief in the pure spirituality of God. Hence Maimonides devoted much of his great treatise, Guide for the Perplexed, to a philosophical allegorisation of the human terms applied to God in the Hebrew Bible. In his Commentary on the Mishnah (Sanhedrin, Introduction to Chelek), Maimonides declares 'The roots of our law and its fundamental principles are thirteen.' These are—(i) Belief in the existence of God, the Creator; (ii) belief in the unity of God; (iii) belief in the incorporeality of God; (iv) belief in the priority and eternity of God; (v) belief that to God and to God alone worship must be offered; (vi) belief in prophecy; (vii) belief that Moses was the greatest of all prophets; (viii) belief that the Law was revealed from heaven; (ix) belief that the Law will never be abrogated, and that no other Law will ever come from God; (x) belief that God knows the works of men; (xi) belief in reward and punishment; (xii) belief in the coming of the Messiah; (xiii) belief in the resurrection of the dead.'

Now here we have for the first time a set of beliefs which were a test of Judaism. Maimonides leaves no doubt as to his meaning. For he concluded by saying: 'When all these principles of faith are in the safe keeping of a man, and his conviction of them is well established, he then enters into the general body of Israel'; and, on the other hand: 'When, however, a man breaks away from any one of these fundamental principles of belief, then of him it is said that he has gone out of the general body of Israel and he denies the root-truths of Judaism.' This formulation of a dogmatic test was never confirmed by any body of Rabbis. No Jew was ever excommunicated for declaring his dissent from these articles. No Jew was ever called upon formally to express his assent to them. But, as Professor Schechter justly writes: 'Among the Maimonists we may probably include the great majority of Jews, who accepted the Thirteen Articles without further question. Maimonides must have filled up a great gap in Jewish theology, a gap, moreover, the existence of which was very generally perceived. A century had hardly lapsed before the Thirteen Articles had become a theme for the poets of the Synagogue. And almost every country can show a poem or a prayer founded on these Articles' (Studies in Judaism, p. 301).

Yet the opposition to the Articles was both impressive and persistent. Some denied altogether the admissibility of Articles, claiming that the whole Law and nothing but the Law was the Charter of Judaism. Others criticised the Maimonist Articles in detail. Certainly they are far from logically drawn up, some paragraphs being dictated by opposition to Islam rather than by positive needs of the Jewish position. A favourite condensation was a smaller list of three Articles: (i) Existence of God; (ii) Revelation; and (iii) Retribution. These three Articles are usually associated with the name of Joseph Albo (1380-1444), though they are somewhat older. There is no doubt but that these Articles found, in recent centuries, more acceptance than the Maimonist Thirteen, though the latter still hold their place in the orthodox Jewish Prayer Books. They may be found in the Authorised Daily Prayer Book, ed. Singer, p. 89.

Moses Mendelssohn (1728-1786), who strongly maintained that Judaism is a life, not a creed, made the practice of formulating Articles of Judaism unfashionable. But not for long. More and more, Judaic ritual has fallen into disregard since the French Revolution. Judaism has therefore tended to express itself as a system of doctrines rather than as a body of practices. And there was a special reason why the Maimonist Articles could not remain. Reference is not meant to the fact that many Jews came to doubt the Mosaic origin of the Pentateuch. But there were lacking in the Maimonist Creed all emotional elements. On the one hand, Maimonides, rationalist and anti-Mystic as he was, makes no allowance for the doctrine of the Immanence of God. Then, owing to his unemotional nature, he laid no stress on all the affecting and moving associations of the belief in the Mission of Israel as the Chosen People. Before Maimonides, if there had been one dogma of Judaism at all, it was the Election of Israel. Jehuda Halevi, the greatest of the Hebrew poets of the Middle Ages, had at the beginning of the twelfth century, some half century before Maimonides, given expression to this in the famous epigram: 'Israel is to the nations like the heart to the limbs.'

Though, however, the Creed of Maimonides has no position of authority in the Synagogue, modern times have witnessed no successful intrusion of a rival. Most writers of treatises on Judaism prefer to describe rather than to define the religious tenets of the faith. In America there have been several suggestions of a Creed. Articles of faith have been there chiefly formulated for the reception of proselytes. This purpose is a natural cause of precision in belief; for while one who already stands within by birth or race is rarely called upon to justify his faith, the newcomer is under the necessity to do so. In the pre-Christian Judaism it is probable that there was a Catechism or short manual of instruction called in Greek the Didache, in which the Golden Rule in Hillel's negative form and the Decalogue occupied a front place. Thus we find, too, modern American Jews formulating Articles of Faith as a Proselyte Confession.

In 1896 the Central Conference of American Rabbis adopted the following five principles for such a Confession: (i) God the Only One; (ii) Man His Image; (iii) Immortality of the Soul; (iv) Retribution; (v) Israel's Mission. During the past few months a tract, entitled 'Essentials of Judaism,' has been issued in London by the Jewish Religious Union. The author, N. S. Joseph, is careful to explain that he is not putting forth these principles as 'dogmatic Articles of Faith,' and that they are solely 'suggestive outlines of belief which may be gradually imparted to children, the outlines being afterwards filled up by the teacher. But the eight paragraphs of these Essentials are at once so ably compiled and so informing as to the modern trend of Jewish belief that they will be here cited without comment.

According then to this presentation, the Essentials of Judaism are: '(i) There is One Eternal God, who is the sole Origin of all things and forces, and the Source of all living souls. He rules the universe with justice, righteousness, mercy, and love. (ii) Our souls, emanating from God, are immortal, and will return to Him when our life on earth ceases. While we are here, our souls can hold direct communion with God in prayer and praise, and in silent contemplation and admiration of His works. (iii) Our souls are directly responsible to God for the work of our life on earth. God, being All-merciful, will judge us with loving-kindness, and being All-just, will allow for our imperfections; and we, therefore, need no mediator and no vicarious atonement to ensure the future welfare of our souls. (iv) God is the One and only God. He is Eternal and Omnipresent. He not only pervades the entire world, but is also within us; and His Spirit helps and leads us towards goodness and truth. (v) Duty should be the moving force of our life; and the thought that God is always in us and about us should incite us to lead good and beneficent lives, showing our love of God by loving our fellow-creatures, and working for their happiness and betterment with all our might. (vi) In various bygone times God has revealed, and even in our own days continues to reveal to us, something of His nature and will, by inspiring the best and wisest minds with noble thoughts and new ideas, to be conveyed to us in words, so that this world may constantly improve and grow happier and better. (vii) Long ago some of our forefathers were thus inspired, and they handed down to us—and through us to the world at large—some of God's choicest gifts, the principles of Religion and Morality, now recorded in our Bible; and these spiritual gifts of God have gradually spread among our fellow-men, so that much of our religion and of its morality has been adopted by them. (viii) Till the main religious and moral principles of Judaism have been accepted by the world at large, the maintenance by the Jews of a separate corporate existence is a religious duty incumbent upon them. They are the "witnesses" of God, and they must adhere to their religion, showing forth its truth and excellence to all mankind. This has been and is and will continue to be their mission. Their public worship and private virtues must be the outward manifestation of the fulfilment of that mission.'

# CHAPTER IV

## SOME CONCEPTS OF JUDAISM

Though there are no accepted Articles of Faith in Judaism, there is a complete consensus of opinion that Monotheism is the basis of the religion. The Unity of God was more than a doctrine. It was associated with the noblest hope of Israel, with Israel's Mission to the world.

The Unity of God was even more than a hope. It was an inspiration, a passion. For it the Jews 'passed through fire and water,' enduring tribulation and death for the sake of the Unity. All the Jewish martyrologies are written round this text.

In one passage the Talmud actually defines the Jew as the
Monotheist. 'Whoever repudiates the service of other gods is called a Jew' (Megillah, 13 a).
But this all-pervading doctrine of the Unity did not reach Judaism as an abstract philosophical truth. Hence, though the belief in the Unity of God, associated as it was with the belief in the Spirituality of God, might have been expected to lead to the conception of an Absolute, Transcendent Being such as we meet in Islam, it did not so lead in Judaism. Judaism never attempted to define God at all. Maimonides put the seal on the reluctance of Jewish theology to go beyond, or to fall short of, what historic Judaism delivered. Judaism wavers between the two opposite conceptions: absolute transcendentalism and absolute pantheism. Sometimes Judaism speaks with the voice of Isaiah; sometimes with the voice of Spinoza. It found the bridge in the Psalter. 'The Lord is nigh unto all that call upon Him.' The Law brought heaven to earth; Prayer raised earth to heaven.

As was remarked above, Jewish theology never shrank from inconsistency. It accepted at once God's foreknowledge and man's free-will. So it described the knowledge of God as far above man's reach; yet it felt God near, sympathetic, a Father and Friend. The liturgy of the Synagogue has been well termed a 'precipitate' of all the Jewish teaching as to God. He is the Great, the Mighty, the Awful, the Most High, the King. But He is also the Father, Helper, Deliverer, the Peace-Maker, Supporter of the weak, Healer of the sick. All human knowledge is a direct manifestation of His grace. Man's body, with all its animal functions, is His handiwork. He created joy, and made the Bridegroom and the Bride. He formed the fruit of the Vine, and is the Source of all the lawful pleasures of men. He is the Righteous Judge; but He remembers that man is dust, He pardons sins, and His loving-kindness is over all. He is unchangeable, yet repentance can avert the evil decree. He is in heaven, yet he puts the love and fear of Him into man's very heart. He breathed the Soul into man, and is faithful to those that sleep in the grave. He is the Reviver of the dead. He is Holy, and He sanctified Israel with His commandments. And the whole is pervaded with the thought of God's Unity and the consequent unity of mankind. Here again we meet the curious syncretism which we have so often observed. God is in a special sense the God of Israel; but He is unequivocally, too, the God of all flesh.

Moses Mendelssohn said that, when in the company of a Christian friend, he never felt the remotest desire to convert him to Judaism. This is the explanation of the effect on the Jews of the combined belief in God as the God of Israel, and also as the God of all men. At one time Judaism was certainly a missionary religion. But after the loss of nationality this quality was practically dormant. Belief was not necessary to salvation. 'The pious of all nations have a part in the world to come' may have been but a casual utterance of an ancient Rabbi, but it rose into a settled conviction of later Judaism. Moreover, it was dangerous for Jews to attempt any religious propaganda in the Middle Ages, and thus the pressure of fact came to the support of theory. Mendelssohn even held that the same religion was not necessarily good for all, just as the same form of government may not fit equally all the various national idiosyncrasies. Judaism for the Jew may almost be claimed as a principle of orthodox Judaism. It says to the outsider: You may come in if you will, but we warn you what it means. At all events it does not seek to attract. It is not strange that this attitude has led to unpopularity. The reason of this resentment is not that men wish to be invited to join Judaism; it lies rather in the sense that the absence of invitation implies an arrogant reserve. To some extent this is the case. The old-fashioned Jew is inclined to think himself superior to other men. Such a thought has its pathos.

On the other hand, the national as contrasted with the universal aspect of Judaism is on the wane. Many Jewish liturgies have, for instance, eliminated the prayers for the restoration of sacrifices; and several have removed or spiritualised the petitions for the recovery of the Jewish nationality. Modern reformed Judaism is a universalistic Judaism. It lays stress on the function of Israel, the Servant, as a 'Light to the Nations.' It tends to eliminate those ceremonies and beliefs which are less compatible with a universal than with, a racial religion. Modern Zionism is not a real reaction against this tendency. For

Zionism is either non-religious or, if religious, brings to the front what has always been a corrective to the nationalism of orthodox Judaism. For the separation of Israel has ever been a means to an end; never an end in itself. Often the end has been forgotten in the means, but never for long. The end of Israel's separateness is the good of the world. And the religious as distinct from the merely political Zionist who thinks that Judaism would gain by a return to Palestine is just the one who also thinks that return is a necessary preliminary to the Messianic Age, when all men shall flow unto Zion and seek God there. Reformed Jews would have to be Zionists also in this sense, were it not that many of them no longer share the belief in the national aspects of the prophecies as to Israel's future. These may believe that the world may become full of the knowledge of God without any antecedent withdrawal of Israel from the world.

If Judaism as a system of doctrine is necessarily syncretistic in its conception of God, then we may expect the same syncretism in its theory of God's relation to man. It must be said at once that the term 'theory' is ill-chosen. It is laid to the charge of Judaism that it has no 'theory' of Sin. This is true. If virtue and righteousness are obedience, then disobedience is both vice and sin. No further theory was required or possible. Atonement is reversion to obedience. Now it was said above that the doctrine of the Unity did not reach Judaism as a philosophical truth exactly defined and apprehended. It came as the result of a long historic groping for the truth, and when it came it brought with it olden anthropomorphic wrappings and tribal adornments which were not easily to be discarded, if they ever were entirely discarded. So with the relation of God to man in general and Israel in particular. The unchangeable God is not susceptible to the change implied in Atonement. But history presented to the Jew examples of what he could not otherwise interpret than as reconciliation between God the Father and Israel the wayward but always at heart loyal Son. And this interpretation was true to the inward experience. Man's repentance was correlated with the sorrow of God. God as well as man repented, the former of punishment, the latter of sin. The process of atonement included contrition, confession, and change of life. Undoubtedly Jewish theology lays the greatest stress on the active stage of the process. Jewish moralists use the word Teshubah (literally 'turning' or 'return,' i.e. a turning from evil or a return to God) chiefly to mean a change of life. Sin is evil life, atonement is the better life. The better life was attained by fasting, prayer, and charity, by a purification of the heart and a cleansing of the hands. The ritual side of atonement was seriously weakened by the loss of the Temple. The sacrificial atonement was gone. Nothing replaced it ritually. Hence the Jewish tendency towards a practical religion was strengthened by its almost enforced stress in atonement on moral betterment. But this moral betterment depended on a renewed communion with God. Sin estranged, atonement brought near. Jewish theology regarded sin as a triumph of the Yetser Ha-ra (the 'evil inclination') over the Yetser Ha-tob (the 'good inclination'). Man was always liable to fall a prey to his lower self. But such a fall, though usual and universal, was not inevitable. Man reasserted his higher self when he curbed his passions, undid the wrong he had wrought to others, and turned again to God with a contrite heart. As a taint of the soul, sin was washed away by the suppliant's tears and confession, by his sense of loss, his bitter consciousness of humiliation, but withal man was helpless without God. God was needed for the atonement. Israel never dreamed of putting forward his righteousness as a claim to pardon. 'We are empty of good works' is the constant refrain of the Jewish penitential appeals. The final reliance is on God and on God alone. Yet Judaism took over from its past the anthropomorphic belief that God could be moved by man's prayers, contrition, amendment—especially by man's amendment. Atonement was only real when the amendment began; it only lasted while the amendment endured. Man must not think to throw his own burden entirely on God. God will help him to bear it, and will lighten the weight from willing shoulders. But bear it man can and must. The shoulders must be at all events willing.

Judaism as a theology stood or fell by its belief that man can affect God. If, for instance, prayer had no validity, then Judaism had no basis. Judaism did not distinguish between the objective and subjective efficacy of prayer. The two went together. The acceptance of the will of God and the inclining of God's purpose to the desire of man were two sides of one fact. The Rabbinic Judaism did not mechanically posit, however, the objective validity of prayer. On the contrary, the man who prayed expecting an answer was regarded as arrogant and sinful. A famous Talmudic prayer sums up the submissive aspect of the Jew in this brief petition (Berachoth, 29 a): 'Do Thy will in heaven above, and grant contentment of spirit to those that fear Thee below; and that which is good in Thine eyes do. Blessed art Thou, O Lord, who hearest prayer.' This, be it remembered, was the prayer of a Pharisee. So, too, a very large portion of all Jewish prayer is not petition but praise. Still, Judaism believed, not that prayer would be answered, but that it could be answered. In modern times the chief cause of the weakening of religion all round, in and out of the Jewish communion, is the growing disbelief in the objective validity of prayer. And a similar remark applies to the belief in miracles. But to a much less extent. All ancient religions were based on miracle, and even to the later religious consciousness a denial of miracle seems to deny the divine Omnipotence.

Jewish theology from the Rabbinic age sought to evade the difficulty by the mystic notion that all miracles were latent in ordered nature at the creation. And so the miraculous becomes interconnected with Providence as revealed in history. But the belief in special miracles recurs again and again in Judaism, and though discarded by most reformed theologies, must be admitted as a prevailing concept of the older religion.

But the belief was rather in general than in special Providence. There was a communal solidarity which made most of the Jewish prayers communal more than personal. It is held by many that in the Psalter 'I' in the majority of cases means the whole people. The sense of brotherhood, in other relations besides public worship, is a perennial characteristic of Judaism.

Even more marked is this in the conception of the family. The hallowing of home-life was one of the best features of Judaism. Chastity was the mark of men and women alike. The position of the Jewish woman was in many ways high. At law she enjoyed certain privileges and suffered certain disabilities. But in the house she was queen. Monogamy had been the rule of Jewish life from the period of the return from the Babylonian Exile. In the Middle Ages the custom of monogamy was legalised in Western Jewish communities. Connected with the fraternity of the Jewish communal organisation and the incomparable affection and mutual devotion of the home-life was the habit of charity. Charity, in the sense both of almsgiving and of loving-kindness, was the virtue of virtues. The very word which in the Hebrew Bible means righteousness means in Rabbinic Hebrew charity. 'On three things the world stands,' says a Rabbi, 'on law, on public worship, and on the bestowal of loving-kindness.'

Some other concepts of Judaism and their influence on character will be treated in a later chapter. Here a final word must be said on the Hallowing of Knowledge.

In one of the oldest prayers of the Synagogue, repeated thrice daily, occurs this paragraph: 'Thou dost graciously bestow on man knowledge, and teachest mortals understanding; O let us be graciously endowed by Thee with knowledge, understanding, and discernment. Blessed art Thou, O Lord, gracious Giver of Knowledge.' The intellect was to be turned to the service of the God from whom intelligence emanated. The Jewish estimate of intellect and learning led to some unamiable contempt of the fool and the ignoramus. But the evil tendency of identifying learning with religion was more than mitigated by the encouragement which this concept gave to education. The ideal was that every Jew must be a scholar, or at all events a student. Obscurantism could not for any lengthy period lodge itself in the Jewish camp. There was no learned caste. The fact that the Bible and much of the most admired literature was in Hebrew made most Jews bilingual at least. But it was not merely that knowledge was useful, that it added dignity to man, and realised part of his possibilities. The service of the Lord called for the dedication of the reason as well as for the purification of the heart. The Jew had to think as well as feel He had to serve with the mind as well as with the body. Therefore it was that he was always anxious to justify his religion to his reason. Maimonides devoted a large section of his Guide to the explanation of the motives of the commandments. And his example was imitated. The Law was the expression of the Will of God, and obeyed and loved as such. But the Law was also the expression of the Divine Reason. Hence man had the right and the duty to examine and realise how his own human reason was satisfied by the Law. In a sense the Jew was a quite simple believer. But never a simpleton. 'Know the Lord thy God' was the key-note of this aspect of Jewish theology.

# CHAPTER V

## SOME OBSERVANCES OF JUDAISM

The historical consciousness of Israel was vitalised by a unique adaptability to present conditions. This is shown in the fidelity with which a number of ancient festivals have been maintained through the ages. Some of these were taken over from pre-Israelite cults. They were nature feasts, and these are among the oldest rites of men. But, as Maimonides wisely said eight centuries ago, religious rites depend not so much on their origins as on the use men make of them. People who wish to return to the primitive usages of this or that church have no grasp of the value and significance of ceremonial. Here, at all events, we are not concerned with origins. The really interesting thing is that feasts, which originated in the fields and under the free heaven, were observed and enjoyed in the confined streets of the Ghetto. The influence of ceremonial is undying when it is bound up with a community's life. 'It is impossible to create festivals to order. One must use those which exist, and where necessary charge them with new meanings.' So writes Mr. Montefiore in his Liberal Judaism (p. 155).

This is precisely what has happened with the Passover, Pentecost, and the Feast of Tabernacles. These three festivals were originally, as has been said, nature feasts. But they became also pilgrim feasts. After the fall of the Temple the pilgrimages to Jerusalem, of course, ceased, and there was an end to the sacrificial rites connected with them all. The only sense in which they can still be called pilgrim feasts is that, despite the general laxity of Sabbath observance and Synagogue attendance, these three celebrations are nowadays occasions on which, in spring, summer, and autumn, a large section of the Jewish community contrives to wend its way to places of public worship.

In the Jewish Liturgy the three feasts have special designations. They are called respectively 'The Season of our Freedom,' 'the Season of the Giving of our Law,' and 'the Season of our Joy.' These descriptions are not biblical, nor are they found in this precise form until the fixation of the Synagogue liturgy in the early part of the Middle Ages. But they have had a powerful influence in perpetuating the hold that the three pilgrim feasts have on the heart and consciousness of Israel. Liberty, Revelation, Joy—these are a sequence of wondrous appeal. Now it is easily seen that these ideas have no indissoluble connection with specific historical traditions. True, 'Freedom' implies the Exodus; 'Revelation,' the Sinaitic theophany; 'Joy,' the harvest merry-makings, and perhaps some connection with the biblical narrative of Israel's wanderings in the wilderness. But the connection, though essential for the construction of the association, is not essential for its retention. 'The Passover,' says Mr. Montefiore (Liberal Judaism, p. 155), 'practically celebrates the formation of the Jewish people. It is also the festival of liberty. In view of these two central features, it does not matter that we no longer believe in the miraculous incidents of the Exodus story. They are mere trappings which can easily be dispensed with. A festival of liberty, the formation of a people for a religious task, a people destined to become a purely religious community whose continued existence has no meaning or value except on the ground of religion,—here we have ideas, which can fitly form the subject of a yearly celebration.' Again, as to Pentecost and the Ten Commandments, Mr. Montefiore writes: 'We do not believe that any divine or miraculous voice, still less that God Himself, audibly pronounced the Ten Words. But their importance lies in themselves, not in their surroundings and origin. Liberals as well as orthodox may therefore join in the festival of the Ten Commandments. Pentecost celebrates the definite union of religion with morality, the inseparable conjunction of the "service" of God with the "service" of man. Can any religious festival have a nobler subject?' Finally, as to tabernacles, Mr. Montefiore thus expresses himself: 'For us, to-day, the connection with the wanderings from Egypt, which the latest [biblical] legislators attempted, has again disappeared. Tabernacles is a harvest festival; it is a nature festival. Should not a religion have a festival or holy day of this kind? Is not the conception of God as the ruler and sustainer of nature, the immanent and all-pervading spirit, one aspect of the Divine, which can fitly be thought of and celebrated year by year? Thus each of the three great Pentateuchal festivals may reasonably and joyfully be observed by liberals and orthodox alike. We have no need or wish to make a change.' And of the actual ceremonial rites connected with the Passover, Pentecost, and Tabernacles, it is apparently only the avoidance of leaven on the first of the three that is regarded as unimportant. But even there Mr. Montefiore's own feeling is in favour of the rite. 'It is,' he says, 'a matter of comparative unimportance whether the practice of eating unleavened bread in the house for the seven days of the Passover be maintained or not. Those who appreciate the value of a pretty and ancient symbol, both for children and adults, will not easily abandon the custom.'

This is surely a remarkable development. In the Christian Church it seems that certain festivals are retaining their general hold because they are becoming public, national holidays. But in Judaism the hold is to be maintained precisely on the ground that there is to be nothing national about them, they are to be reinterpreted ideally and symbolically. It remains to be seen whether this is possible, and it is too early to predict the verdict of experience. The process is in active incubation in America as well as in Europe, but it cannot be claimed that the eggs are hatched yet. On the other hand, Zionism has so far had no effect in the opposite direction. There has been no nationalization of Judaism as a result of the new striving after political nationality. Many who had previously been detached from the Jewish community have been brought back by Zionism, but they have not been re-attached to the religion. There has been no perceptible increase, for instance, in the number of those who fast on the Ninth of Ab, the anniversary of the destruction of the Temple. Hence, from these and other considerations, of which limited space prevents the specification, it seems on the whole likely that, as in the past so in the future, the Festivals of the Synagogue will survive by changes in religious significance rather than by any deepening of national association.

Except that the Synagogues are decked with flowers, while the Decalogue is solemnly intoned from the Scroll of the Pentateuch, the Feast of Pentecost has no ceremonial trappings even with the orthodox. Passover and Tabernacles stand on a different footing. The abstention from leavened bread on the former feast has led to a closely organised system of cleansing the houses, an interminable array of rules as to food; while the prescriptions of the Law as to the bearing of palm-branches and other emblems, and the ordinance as to dwelling in booths, have surrounded the Feast of Tabernacles with a considerable, if less extensive, ceremonial. But there is this difference. The Passover is primarily a festival of the Home, Tabernacles of the Synagogue. In Europe the habit of actually dwelling in booths has been long unusual, owing to climatic considerations. But of late years it has become customary for every Synagogue to raise its communal booth, to which many Jews pay visits of ceremony. On the other hand, the Passover is par excellence a home rite. On the first two evenings (or at all events on the first evening) there takes place the Seder, (literally 'service'), a service of prayer, which is at the same time a family meal. Gathered round the table, on which are spread unleavened cakes, bitter herbs, and other emblems of joy and sorrow, the family recounts in prose and song the narrative of the Exodus. The service is in two parts, between which comes the evening meal. The hallowing of the home here attains its highest point.

Unless, indeed, this distinction be allotted to the Sabbath. The rigidity of the laws regarding Sabbath observance is undeniable. Movement was restricted, many acts were forbidden which were not in themselves laborious. The

Sabbath was hedged in by a formidable array of enactments. To an outside critic it is not wonderful that the Jewish Sabbath has a repellent look. But to the insider things wear another aspect. The Sabbath was and is a day of delight. On it the Jew had a foretaste of the happiness of the world to come. The reader who wishes to have a spirited, and absolutely true, picture of the Jewish Sabbath cannot do better than turn to Dr. Schechter's excellent Studies in Judaism (pp. 296 seq.). As Dr. Schechter pithily puts it: 'Somebody, either the learned professors, or the millions of the Jewish people, must be under a delusion.' Right through the Middle Ages the Sabbath grew deeper into the affections of the Jews. It was not till after the French Revolution and the era of emancipation, which a change occurred. Mixing with the world, and sharing the world's pursuits, the Jews began to find it hard to observe the Saturday Sabbath as of old. In still more recent times the difficulty has increased. Added to this, the growing laxity in observances has affected the Sabbath. This is one of the most pressing problems that face the Jewish community to-day. Here and there an attempt has been made by small sections of Jews to substitute a Sunday Sabbath for the Saturday Sabbath. But the plan has not prospered.

One of the most notable rites of the Service of the Passover eve is the sanctification with wine, a ceremony common to the ordinary Sabbath eve. This rite has perhaps had much to do with the characteristic sobriety of Israel. Wine forms part of almost every Jewish rite, including the marriage ceremony. Wine thus becomes associated with religion, and undue indulgence is a sin as well as a vice. 'No joy without wine,' runs an old Rabbinic prescription. Joy is the hallmark of Judaism; 'Joyous Service' its summary of man's relation to the Law. So far is Judaism from being a gloomy religion, that it is almost too light-hearted, just as was the religion of ancient Greece. But the Talmud tells us of a class who in the early part of the first century were known as 'lovers of sorrow.' These men were in love with misfortune; for to every trial of Israel corresponded an intervention of the divine salvation. This is the secret of the Jewish gaiety. The resilience under tribulation was the result of a firm confidence in the saving fidelity of God. And the gaiety was tempered by solemnity, as the observances, to which we now turn, will amply show.

Far more remarkable than anything yet discussed is the change effected in two other holy days since Bible times. The genius of Judaism is nowhere more conspicuous than in the fuller meanings which have been infused into the New Year's Day and the Day of Atonement. The New Year is the first day of the seventh month (Tishri), when the ecclesiastical year began. In the Bible the festival is only known as a 'day of blowing the shofar' (ram's horn). In the

Synagogue this rite was retained after the destruction of the Temple, and it still is universally observed. But the day was transformed into a Day of Judgment, the opening of a ten days' period of Penitence which closed with the Day of Atonement.

Here, too, the change effected in a biblical rite transformed its character. 'It needed a long upward development before a day, originally instituted on priestly ideas of national sin and collective atonement, could be transformed into the purely spiritual festival which we celebrate to-day' (Montefiore, op. cit., p. 160). But the day is none the less associated with a strict rite, the fast. It is one of the few ascetic ceremonies in the Jewish Calendar as known to most Jews. There is a strain of asceticism in some forms of Judaism, and on this a few words will be said later. But, on the whole, there is in modern Judaism a tendency to underrate somewhat the value of asceticism in religion. Hence the fast has a distinct importance in and for itself, and it is regrettable that the laudable desire to spiritualise the day is leading to a depreciation of the fast as such. But the real change is due to the cessation of sacrifices. In the Levitical Code, sacrifice had a primary importance in the scheme of atonement. But with the loss of the Temple, the idea of sacrifice entirely vanished, and atonement became a matter for the personal conscience. It was henceforth an inward sense of sin translating itself into the better life. 'To purify desire, to ennoble the will—this is the essential condition of atonement. Nay, it is atonement' (Joseph, Judaism as Creed and Life, p. 267; cf. supra, p. 45). This, in the opinion of Christian theologians, is a shallow view of atonement. But it is at all events an attempt to apply theology to life. And its justification lies in its success.

Of the other festivals a word is due concerning two of them, which differ much in significance and in development. Purim and Chanuka are their names. Purim was probably the ancient Babylonian Saturnalia, and it is still observed as a kind of Carnival by many Jews, though their number is decreasing. For Purim is emphatically a Ghetto feast. And this description applies in more ways than one. In the first place, the Book of Esther, with which the Jewish Purim is associated, is not a book that commends itself to the modern Jewish consciousness. The historicity of the story is doubted, and its narrow outlook is not that of prophetic Judaism. Observed as mediaeval Jews observed it, Purim was a thoroughly innocent festivity. The unpleasant taste left by the closing scenes of the book was washed off by the geniality of temper which saw the humours of Haman's fall and never for a moment rested in a feeling of vindictiveness. But the whole book breathes so nationalistic a spirit, so uncompromising a belief that the enemy of Israel must be the enemy of God, that it has become difficult for modern Judaism to retain any affection for it. It makes its appeal to the persecuted, no doubt: it conveys a stirring lesson in the providential care with which God watches over His people: it bids the sufferer hope. Esther's splendid surrender of self, her immortal declaration, 'If I perish, I perish,' still may legitimately thrill all hearts. But the Carnival has no place in the life of a Western city, still less the sectional Carnival. The hobby-horse had its opportunity and the maskers their rights in the Ghetto, but only there. Purim thus is now chiefly retained as a children's feast, and still better as a feast of charity, of the interchange of gifts between friends, and the bestowal of alms on the needy. This is a worthy survival.

Chanuka, on the other hand, grows every year into greater popularity. This festival of light, when lamps are kindled in honour of the Maccabean heroes, has of late been rediscovered by the liberals. For the first four centuries of the Christian Era, the festival of Chanuka ('Dedication') was observed by the Church as well as by the Synagogue. But for some centuries afterwards the significance of the anniversary was obscured. It is now realised as a momentous event in the world's history. It was not merely a local triumph of Hebraism over Hellenism, but it represents the re-entry of the East into the civilisation of the West. Alexander the Great had occidentalised the Orient. But with the success of the Judaeans against the Seleucids and of the Parthians against the Romans, the East reasserted itself. And the newly recovered influence has never again been surrendered. Hence this feast is a feast of ideals. Year by year this is becoming more clearly seen. And the symbol of the feast, light, is itself an inspiration.

The Jew is really a very sentimental being. He loves symbols. A good deal of his fondness for ritual is due to this fact. The outward marks of an inner state have always appealed to him. Ancient taboos became not only consecrated but symbolical. Whether it be the rite of circumcision, or the use of phylacteries and fringed praying garments, or the adfixture of little scrolls in metal cases on the door-posts, or the glad submission to the dietary laws, in all these matters sentiment played a considerable part. And the word sentiment is used in its best sense. Abstract morality is well enough for the philosopher, but men of flesh and blood want their morality expressed in terms of feeling. Love of God is a fine thing, but the Jew wished to do loving acts of service. Obedience to the Will of God, the suppression of the human desires before that Will, is a great ideal. But the Jew wished to realise that he was obeying, that he was making the self-suppression. He was not satisfied with a general law of holiness: he felt impelled to holiness in detail, to a life in which the laws of bodily hygiene were obeyed as part of the same law of holiness that imposed ritual and moral purity. Much of the intricate system, of observance briefly summarised in this paragraph, a system which filled the Jew's life, is passing away. This is largely because Jews are surrendering their own original theory of life and religion. Modern Judaism seems to have no use for the ritual system. The older Judaism might retort that, if that be so, it has no use for the modern Judaism. It is, however, clear that modern Judaism now realises the mistake made by the Reformers of the mid-nineteenth century. Hence we are hearing, and shall no doubt hear more and more, of the modification of observances in Judaism rather than of their abolition.

# CHAPTER VI

## JEWISH MYSTICISM

'Judaism is often called the religion of reason. It is this, but it is also the religion of the soul. It recognises the value of that mystic insight, those indefinable intuitions which, taking up the task at the point where the mind impotently abandons it, carries us straight into the presence of the King. Thus it has found room both for the keen speculator on theological problems and for the mystic who, because he feels God, declines to reason about Him—for a Maimonides and a Mendelssohn, but also for a Nachmanides, a Vital, and a Luria' (M. Joseph, op. cit., p. 47). Used in a vague way, mysticism stands for spiritual inwardness. Religion without mysticism, said Amiel, is a rose without perfume. This saying is no more precise and no more informing than Matthew Arnold's definition of religion as morality touched with emotion. Neither mysticism nor an emotional touch makes religion. They are as often as not concomitants of a pathological state which is the denial of religion. But if mysticism means a personal attitude towards God in which the heart is active as well as the mind, then religion cannot exist without mysticism.

When, however, we regard mysticism as what it very often is, as an antithesis to institutional religion and a revolt against authority and forms, then it may seem at first sight paradoxical to recognise the mystic's claim to the hospitality of Judaism. That a religion which produced the Psalter, and not only produced it, but used it with never a break, should be a religion, with intensely spiritual possibilities, and its adherents capable of a vivid sense of the nearness of God, with an ever-felt and never-satisfied longing for communion with Him, is what we should fully expect. But this expectation would rather make us look for an expression on the lines of the 119th Psalm, in which the Law is so markedly associated with freedom and spirituality. Judaism, after all, allowed to authority and Law a supreme place. But the mystic relies on his own intuitions, depends on his personal experiences. Judaism, on the other hand, is a scheme in which personal experiences only count in so far as they are brought into the general fund of the communal experience.

But in discussing Judaism it is always imperative to discard all a priori probabilities. Judaism is the great upsetter of the probable. Analyse a tendency of Judaism and predict its logical consequences, and then look in Judaism for consequences quite other than these. Over and over again things are not what they ought to be. The sacrificial system should have destroyed spirituality; in fact, it produced the Psalter, 'the hymnbook of the second Temple.' Pharisaism ought to have led to externalism; in fact, it did not, for somehow excessive scrupulosity in rite and pietistic exercises went hand in hand with simple faith and religious inwardness. So, too, the expression of ethics and religion as Law ought to have suppressed individuality; in fact, it sometimes gave an impulse to each individual to try to impose his own concepts, norms, and acts as a Law upon the rest. Each thought very much for himself, and desired that others should think likewise. We have already seen that in matters of dogma there never was any corporate action at all; in ancient times, as now, it is not possible to pronounce definitely on the dogmatic teachings of Judaism. Though there has been and is a certain consensus of opinion on many matters, yet neither in practice nor in beliefs have the local, the temporal, the personal elements ever been negligible. In order to expound or define a tenet or rite of Judaism it is mostly necessary to go into questions of time and place and person.

Perhaps, then, we ought to be prepared to find, as in point of fact we do find, within the main body of Judaism, and not merely as a freak of occasional eccentrics, distinct mystical tendencies. These tendencies have often been active well inside the sphere of the Law. Mysticism was, as we shall see, sometimes a revolt against Law; but it was often, in Judaism as in the Roman Catholic Church, the outcome of a sincere and even passionate devotion to authority. Jewish mysticism, in particular, starts as an interpretation of the Scriptures. Certain truths were arrived at by man either intuitively or rationally, and these were harmonised with the Bible by a process of lifting the veil from the text, and thus penetrating to the true meaning hidden beneath the letter. Allegorical and esoteric exegesis always had this aim: to find written what had been otherwise found. Honour was thus done to the Scriptures, though the latter were somewhat cavalierly treated in the process; Philo's doctrine (at the beginning of the Christian era) and the great canonical book of the mediaeval Cabbala, the Zohar (beginning of the fourteenth century), were alike in this, they were largely commentaries on the Pentateuch. Maimonides in the twelfth century followed the same method, and only differed from these in the nature of his deductions from Scripture. This prince of rationalists agreed with the mystics in adopting an esoteric exegesis. But he read Aristotle into the text, while the mystics read Plato into it. They were alike faithful to the Law, or rather to their own interpretations of its terms.

But further than this,—a large portion of Jewish mysticism was the work of lawyers. Some of the foremost mystics were famous Talmudists, men who were appealed to for decisions on ritual and conduct. It is a phenomenon that constantly meets us in Jewish theology. There were antinomian mystics and legalistic opponents of mysticism, but many, like Nachmanides (1195-1270) and Joseph Caro (1488-1575), doubled the parts of Cabbalist and Talmudist. That Jewish mysticism comes to look like a revolt against the Talmud is due to the course of mediaeval scholasticism. While Aristotle was supreme, it was impossible for man to conceive as knowable anything unattainable by reason. But reason must always leave God as unknowable. Mysticism did not assert that God was knowable, but it substituted something else for this spiritual scepticism. Mysticism started with the conviction that God was unknowable by reason, but it held that God was nevertheless realisable in the human experience. Accepting and adopting various Neo-Platonic theories of emanation, elaborating thence an intricate angelology, the mystics threw a bridge over the gulf between God and man. Philo's Logos, the Personified Wisdom of the Palestinian Midrash, the demiurge of Gnosticism, the incarnate Christ, were all but various phases of this same attempt to cross an otherwise impassable chasm. Throughout its whole history, Jewish mysticism substituted mediate creation for immediate creation out of nothing, and the mediate beings were not created but were emanations. This view was much influenced by Solomon ibn Gabirol (1021-1070). God is to Gabirol an absolute Unity, in which form and substance are identical. Hence He cannot be attributively defined, and man can know Him only by means of beings which emanate from Him. Nor was this idea confined to Jewish philosophy of the Greece-Arabic school. The German Cabbala, too, which owed nothing directly to that school, held that God was not rationally knowable. The result must be, not merely to exalt visionary meditation over calm ratiocination, but to place reliance on inward experience instead of on external authority, which makes its appeal necessarily to the reason. Here we see elements of revolt. For, as Dr. L. Ginzberg well says, 'while study of the Law was to Talmudists the very acme of piety, the mystics accorded the first place to prayer, which was considered as a mystical progress towards God, demanding a state of ecstasy.' The Jewish mystic must invent means for inducing such a state, for Judaism cannot endure a passive waiting for the moving spirit. The mystic soul must learn how to mount the chariot (Merkaba) and ride into the inmost halls of Heaven. Mostly the ecstatic state was induced by fasting and other ascetic exercises, a necessary preliminary being moral purity; then there were solitary meditations and long night vigils; lastly, prescribed ritual of proved efficacy during the very act of prayer. Thus mysticism had a farther attraction for a certain class of Jews, in that it supplied the missing element of asceticism which is indispensable to men more austerely disposed than the average Jew.

In the sixteenth century a very strong impetus was given to Jewish mysticism by Isaac Luria (1534-1572). His chief contributions to the movement were practical, though he doubtless taught a theoretical Cabbala also. But Judaism, even in its mystical phases, remains a religion of conduct. Luria was convinced that man can conquer matter; this practical conviction was the moving force of his whole life. His own manner of living was saintly; and he taught his disciples that they too could, by penitence, confession, prayer, and charity, evade bodily trammels and send their souls straight to God even during their terrestrial pilgrimage. Luria taught all this not only while submitting to Law, but under the stress of a passionate submission to it. He added in particular a new beauty to the Sabbath. Many of the most fascinatingly religious rites connected now with the Sabbath are of his devising. The white Sabbath garb, the joyous mystical hymns full of the Bride and of Love, the special Sabbath foods, the notion of the 'over-Soul'—these and many other of the Lurian rites and fancies still hold wide sway in the Orient. The 'over-Soul' was a very inspiring conception, which certainly did not originate with Luria. According to a Talmudic Rabbi (Resh Lakish, third century), on Adam was bestowed a higher soul on the Sabbath, which he lost at the close of the day. Luria seized upon this mystical idea, and used it at once to spiritualise the Sabbath and attach to it an ecstatic joyousness. The ritual of the 'over-Soul' was an elaborate means by which a relation was established between heaven and earth. But all this symbolism had but the slightest connection with dogma. It was practical through and through. It emerged in a number of new rites, it based itself on and became the cause of a deepening devotion to morality. Luria would have looked with dismay on the moral laxity which did later on intrude, in consequence of unbridled emotionalism and mystic hysteria. There comes the point when he that interprets Law emotionally is no longer Law-abiding. The antinomian crisis thus produced meets us in the careers of many who, like Sabbatai Zebi, assumed the Messianic role.

Jewish mysticism, starting as an ascetic corrective to the conventional hedonism, lost its ascetic character and degenerated into licentiousness. This was the case with the eighteenth-century mysticism known as Chassidism, though, as its name ('Saintliness') implies, it was innocent enough at its initiation. Violent dances, and other emotional and sensual stimulations, led to a state of exaltation during which the line of morality was overstepped. But there was nevertheless, as Dr. Schechter has shown, considerable spiritual worth and beauty in Chassidism. It transferred the centre of gravity from thinking to feeling; it led away from the worship of Scripture to the love of God.

The fresh air of religion was breathed once more, the stars and the open sky replaced the midnight lamp and the college. But it was destined to raise a fog more murky than the confined atmosphere of the study. The man with the book was often nearer God than was the man of the earth.

The opposition of Talmudism against the neo-mysticism was thus on the whole just and salutary. This opposition, no doubt, was bitter chiefly when mysticism became revolutionary in practice, when it invaded the established customs of legalistic orthodoxy. But it was also felt that mysticism went dangerously near to a denial of the absolute Unity of God. It was more difficult to attack it on its theoretical than on its practical side, however. The Jewish mystic did sometimes adopt a most irritating policy of deliberately altering customs as though for the very pleasure of change. Now in most religious controversies discipline counts for more than belief. As Salimbene asserts of his own day: 'It was far less dangerous to debate in the schools whether God really existed, than to wear publicly and pertinaciously a frock and cowl of any but the orthodox cut.' But the Talmudists' antagonism to mysticism was not exclusively of this kind in the eighteenth century. Mysticism is often mere delusion. In the last resort man has no other guide than his reason. It is his own reason that convinces him of the limitations of his reason. But those limitations are not to be overpassed by a visionary self-introspection, unless this, too, is subjected to rational criticism. Mysticism does its true part when it applies this criticism also to the current forms, conventions, and institutions. Conventions, forms, and institutions, after all, represent the corporate wisdom, the accumulated experiences of men throughout the ages. Mysticism is the experience of one. Each does right to test the corporate experience by his own experience. But he must not elevate himself into a law even for himself. That, in a sentence, would summarise the attitude of Judaism towards mysticism. It is medicine, not a food.

# CHAPTER VII

# ESCHATOLOGY

That the soul has a life of its own after death was a firmly fixed idea in Judaism, though, except in the works of philosophers and in the liberal theology of modern Judaism, the grosser conception of a bodily Resurrection was predominant over the purely spiritual idea of Immortality. Curiously enough, Maimonides, who formulated the belief in Resurrection as a dogma of the Synagogue, himself held that the world to come is altogether free from material factors. At a much earlier period (in the third century) Rab had said (Ber. 17 a): 'Not as this world is the world to come. In the world to come there is no eating or drinking, no sexual intercourse, no barter, no envy, hatred, or contention. But the righteous sit with their crowns on their heads, enjoying the splendour of the Shechinah (the Divine Presence).' Commenting on this in various places, Maimonides emphatically asserts the spirituality of the future life. In his Siraj he says, with reference to the utterance of Rab just quoted: 'By the remark of the Sages "with their crowns on their heads" is meant the preservation of the soul in the intellectual sphere, and the merging of the two into one.... By their remark "enjoying the splendour of the Shechinah" is meant that those souls will reap bliss in what they comprehend of the Creator, just as the Angels enjoy felicity in what they understand of His existence. And so the felicity and the final goal consists in reaching to this exalted company and attaining this high pitch.' Again, in his philosophical Guide (I. xli.), Maimonides distinguishes three kinds of 'soul': (1) The principle of animality, (2) the principle of humanity, and (3) the principle of intellectuality, that part of man's individuality which can exist independently of the body, and therefore alone survives death. Even more remarkable is the fact that Maimonides enunciates the same opinion in his Code (Laws of Repentance, viii. 2). For the Code differs from the other two of the three main works of Maimonides in that it is less personal, and expresses what the author conceives to be the general opinion of Judaism as interpreted by its most authoritative teachers.

There can be no question but that this repeated insistence of Maimonides has strongly affected all subsequent Jewish thought. To him, eternal bliss consists in perfect spiritual communion with God. 'He who desires to serve God from Love must not serve to win the future world. But he does right and eschews wrong because he is man, and owes it to his manhood to perfect himself. This effort brings him to the type of perfect man, whose soul shall live in the state that befits it, viz. in the world to come.' Thus the world to come is a state rather than a place.

But Maimonides' view was not accepted without dispute. It was indeed quite easy to cite Rabbinic passages in which the world to come is identified with the bodily Resurrection. Against Maimonides were produced such Talmudic utterances as the following: 'Said Rabbi Chiya b. Joseph, the Righteous shall arise clad in their garments, for if a grain of wheat which is buried naked comes forth with many garments, how much more shall the righteous arise full garbed, seeing that they were interred with shrouds' (Kethub. 111 b). Again, 'Rabbi Jannai said to his children, Bury me not in white garments or in black: not in white, lest I be not held worthy (of heaven) and thus may be like a bridegroom among mourners (in Gehenna); nor in black, lest if I am held worthy, I be like a mourner among bridegrooms (in heaven). But bury me in coloured garments (so that my appearance will be partly in keeping with either fate),' (Sabbath, 114 a). Or finally: 'They arise with their blemishes, and then are healed' (Sanh. 91 b).

The popular fancy, in its natural longing for a personal existence after the bodily death, certainly seized upon the belief in Resurrection with avidity. It had its roots partly in the individual consciousness, partly in the communal. For the Resurrection was closely connected with such hopes as those expressed in Ezekiel's vision of the re-animation of Israel's dry bones (Ezek. xxxvii.). Thus popular theology adopted many ideas based on the Resurrection. The myth of the Leviathan hardly belongs here, for, widespread as it was, it was certainly not regarded in a material light. The Leviathan was created on the fifth day, and its flesh will be served as a banquet for the righteous at the advent of Messiah. The mediaeval poets found much attraction in this idea, and allowed their imagination full play concerning the details of the divine repast. Maimonides entirely spiritualised the idea, and his example was here decisive. The conception of the Resurrection had other consequences. As the scene of the Resurrection is to be Jerusalem, there grew up a strong desire to be buried on the western slope of Mount Olivet. In fact, many burial and mourning customs of the Synagogue originated from a belief in the bodily Resurrection. But even in the orthodox liturgy the direct references to it are vague and idealised. Two passages of great beauty may be cited. The first is taken from the Authorised Daily Prayer Book (ed. Singer, p. 5):

'O my God, the soul which Thou gavest me is pure; Thou didst create it, Thou didst form it, Thou didst breathe it into me; Thou preservest it within me; and

Thou wilt take it from me, but wilt restore it unto me hereafter. So long as the soul is within me, I will give thanks unto Thee, O Lord my God and God of my fathers, Sovereign of all works, Lord of all souls! Blessed art Thou, O Lord, who restorest souls unto dead bodies.' The last phrase is also extant in another reading in the Talmud and in some liturgies: 'Blessed art Thou, who revivest the dead,' but the meaning of the two forms is identical. This passage, be it noted, is ancient, and is recited every morning at prayer. The second passage is recited even more frequently, for it is said thrice daily, and also forms part of the funeral service. It may be found in the Prayer Book just quoted on p. 44: 'Thou, O Lord, art mighty for ever, Thou quickenest the dead, Thou art mighty to save. Thou sustainest the living with loving-kindness, quickenest the dead with great mercy, supportest the falling, healest the sick, loosest the bound, and keepest Thy faith to them that sleep in the dust. Who is like unto Thee, Lord of mighty acts, and who resembleth Thee, O King, who killest and quickenest, and causest salvation to spring forth? Yea faithful art Thou to quicken the dead.'

The later history of the doctrine in the Synagogue may be best summarised in the words of Dr. Kohler, whose theological articles in the Jewish Encyclopedia deserve grateful recognition. What follows may be read at full length in that work, vol. vi. p. 567: 'While mediaeval philosophy dwelt on the intellectual, moral, or spiritual nature of the soul to prove its immortality, the Cabbalists endeavoured to explain the soul as a light from heaven, after Proverbs xx. 27, and immortality as a return to the celestial world of pure light. But the belief in the pre-existence of the soul led the mystics to the adoption, with all its weird notions and superstitions, of the Pythagorean system of the transmigration of the soul.' Moses Mendelssohn revived the Platonic form of the doctrine of immortality. Thenceforth the dogma of the Resurrection was gradually discarded until it was eliminated from the Prayer Book of the Reform congregations. Man's future was thought of as the realisation of those 'higher expectations which are sown, as part of its very nature, in every human soul.' The statement of Genesis that 'God made man in His own image,' and the idea conveyed in the text (1 Samuel xxv. 29), 'May the soul ... be bound up in the bundle of life with the Lord thy God,' which as a divine promise and a human supplication 'filled the generations with comfort and hope, received a new meaning from this view of man's future; and the Rabbinical saying (Ber. 64 a): "The Righteous rest not, either in this or in the future world, but go from strength to strength until they see God in Zion," appeared to offer an endless vista to the hope of immortality.'

But quite apart from this indefiniteness of attitude as to the meaning of immortality, it is scarcely possible to speak of a Jewish Eschatology at all. The development of an Eschatology occurred in that section of Jewish opinion which remained on the fringe. It must be sought in the apocalyptic literature, which has been preserved in Greek. The whole subject had but a small attraction for Judaism proper. Naturally there was some curiosity and some speculation. The Day of the Lord, with its combination of Retribution and Salvation, was pictured in various ways and with some elaboration of detail. Paradise and Hell were mapped out, and the comfortable compartments to be occupied by the saints and the miserable quarters of sinners were specified with the precision of an Ordnance Survey. Purgatory was an institution not limited to the Roman Catholic Church; it had a strong hold on the mediaeval Jewish mind. The intermediate state was a favourite escape from the theological necessity of condemning sinners to eternal punishment. The Jewish heart could not suffer the pain of conceiving Gehenna inevitable. So, one by one, those who might logically be committed there were rescued on various pretexts. In the end the number of the individual sinners who were to suffer eternal torture could be named on the fingers of one hand.

By the preceding paragraph it is not implied that Jewish literature in Hebrew has not its full complement of fancies, horrible and beautiful, regarding heaven and hell. But such fancies were neither dogmatic nor popular. They never found their way into the tenets of Judaism as formulated by any authority; they never became a moving power in the life of the Jewish masses. It was the poets who nourished these lurid ideas, and poetry which has done so much for the good of religion has also done it many a disservice. Judaism, in its prosaic form, accepted the ideas of Immortality, Retribution, and so forth, but the real interest was in life here, not in life hereafter.

We can see how the two were bridged over by the Jewish conviction of human solidarity. For twelve months after the death of a father the son recited daily the Kaddish prayer (Authorised Daily Prayer Book, p. 77). This was a mere Doxology, opening: 'Magnified and sanctified be His great name in the world which He hath created according to His will. May He establish His kingdom during your life and during your days, and during the life of all the house of Israel, even speedily and at a near time, and say ye Amen.' As to the Messianic idea of the Kingdom of God, something will be said in the next chapter. But this Doxology was believed efficacious to save the departed soul when uttered by the living son. The generations were thus bound together, and just as the merits of the fathers could exert benign influence over the erring child on earth, so could the praises of the child move the mercy of God in favour of the erring father in Purgatory. It was a beautiful expression of the unbreakable chain of tradition, a tradition whose links were human hearts. In such conceptions, rather than in descriptive pictures of Paradise and Gehenna, is the true mind of Judaism to be discerned.

That the first formal sign of grief at the death of a parent should be a Doxology will not have escaped notice. God is the Righteous Judge. Thus, in the Eschatology of Judaism, this idea of Judgment predominates. A favourite passage was the Mishnic utterance (second century): 'Rabbi Eleazar said: They that are born are destined to die, and they that die to be brought to life again, and they that live to be judged.' (Aboth, iv. 29). But in another sense, too, there was judgment at death. The sorrow of the survivors, like the decease of the departed, was to be considered as God's doing, and therefore right. Hence in the very moment of the death of a loved one, when grief was most poignant, the survivor stood forth before the congregation and praised God. And so the Burial Service is named in Hebrew 'Zidduk Ha-din,' i.e. 'The Justification of the Judgment.' A few sentences in it ran thus (Prayer Book, p. 318): 'The Rock, His work is perfect.... He ruleth below and above, He bringeth down to the grave and bringeth up again.... Blessed be the true Judge.' And perhaps more than all attempts to analyse beliefs and dogmas, the following prayer, recited during the week of mourning for the dead, will convey to the reader the real attitude of Judaism (at least in its central variety) to some of the questions which have occupied us in this chapter. The quotation is made from of the same Prayer Book that has been already cited several times above:

'O Lord and King, who art full of compassion, in whose hand is the soul of every living thing and the breath of all flesh, who killest and makest alive, who bringest down to the grave and bringest up again, receive, we beseech Thee, in Thy great loving-kindness, the soul of our brother who hath been gathered unto his people. Have mercy upon him, pardon all his transgressions, for there is not a righteous man upon earth, who doeth good and sinneth not. Remember unto him the righteousness which he wrought, and let his reward be with him and his recompense before him. O shelter his soul in the shadow of Thy wings. Make known to Him the path of life: in Thy presence is fulness of joy; at Thy right hand are pleasures for evermore. Vouchsafe unto him of the abounding happiness that is treasured up for the righteous, as it is written, Oh how great is Thy goodness, which Thou hast laid up for them that fear Thee, which Thou hast wrought for them that trust in Thee before the children of men!

'O Lord, who healest the broken-hearted and bindest up their wounds, grant Thy consolation unto the mourners: put into their hearts the fear and love of Thee, that they may serve Thee with a perfect heart, and let their latter end be peace.

'Like one whom his mother comforteth, so will I comfort you, and in Jerusalem shall ye be comforted. Thy sun shall no more go down, neither shall thy moon withdraw itself; for the Lord shall be thine everlasting light, and the days of thy mourning shall be ended.

'He will destroy death for ever; and the Lord will wipe away tears from off all faces; and the rebuke of his people shall he take away from off all the earth: for the Lord hath spoken it.'

# CHAPTER VIII

## THE SURVIVAL OF JUDAISM

The Messianic Hope has an intimate connection with Eschatology. Whereas, however, the latter in so far as it affirmed a Resurrection conceived of the immortality of Israelites, the former conceived the Immortality of Israel. It is not necessary here to trace the origin and history of the Messianic idea in Judaism. That this idea had a strong nationalistic tinge is obvious. The Messiah was to be a person of Davidic descent, who would be the restorer of Israel's greatness. Throughout Jewish history, despite the constant injunction to refrain 'from calculating the date of the end,' men have arisen who have claimed to be Messiahs, and these have mostly asserted their claim on nationalistic pleas. They were to be kings of Israel as well as inaugurators of a new regime of moral and spiritual life. But though this is true without qualification, it is equally true that the philosophers of the Middle Ages tried to remove all materialistic notions from the Messianic idea. It is very difficult to assert nowadays whether Judaism does or does not expect a personal Messiah. A very marked change has undoubtedly come over the spirit of the dream.

On the one hand the neo-Nationalists deny any Messianic hopes. When that great leader, Theodor Herzl, started a Zionistic movement without claiming to be the Jewish Messiah, he was putting the seal on a far-reaching change in Jewish sentiment. Dr. J. H. Greenstone, who has just published an interesting volume on the Messianic Idea in Jewish History, writes (p. 276): 'After the first Basle Congress (1897), when Zionism assumed its present political aspect, Dr. Max Nordau, the vice-president of the Congress, found it necessary to address an article to the Hebrew-reading public, in which he disclaimed all pretensions of Messiahship for himself or for his colleague Dr. Theodor Herzl.' We have thus this extraordinary situation. Many orthodox Jews stood aloof from the Zionistic movement because it was not Messianic, while many unorthodox Jews joined it just because of the movement's detachment from Messianic ideas.

It may be well to cite Dr. Greenstone's verdict on the whole question, as the reader may care to have the opinion of so competent an authority whose view differs from that of the present writer. 'Sacred as Zionism is to many of its adherents, it cannot and will not take the place of the Messianic hope. Zionism aims at the establishment of a Jewish State in Palestine under the protection of the powers of Europe. The Messianic hope promises the establishment, by the Jews, of a world-power in Palestine to which all the nations of the earth will pay homage. Zionism, even in its political aspect, will fulfil only one phase of the Jewish Messianic hope. As such, if successful, it may contribute toward the full realisation of the hope. If not successful, it will not deprive the Jews of the hope. The Messianic hope is wider than the emancipation of the Jews, it is more comprehensive than the establishment of a Jewish, politically independent State. It participates in the larger ideals of humanity, the ideals of perfection for the human race, but it remains on Jewish soil, and retains its peculiarly Jewish significance. It promises universal peace, an age of justice and of righteousness, an age in which all men will recognise that God is One and His name One. But this glorious age will come about through the regeneration of the Jewish people, which in turn be effected by a man, a scion of the house of David, sent by God to guide them on the road to righteousness. The people chosen by God to be His messengers to the world will then be able to accomplish their mission of regenerating the world. This was the Messianic hope proclaimed by the prophets and sages, and this is the Messianic hope of most Jews to-day, the difference between the various sections being only a difference in the details of the hope' (op. cit., p. 278).

Dr. Greenstone surely cannot mean that the question of a 'personal Messiah' is a mere detail of the belief. Yet it is on that point that opinion is most divided among Jews. The older belief undeniably was what Dr. Greenstone enunciates. But for this belief, none of what Mr. Zangwill aptly terms the 'Dreamers of the Ghetto' would have found the ready acceptance that several of them did when they presented themselves as Messiah or his forerunners. And no doubt there are many Jews who still cling to this form of the belief.

On the other hand, there has been a slow but widespread tendency to reinterpret the whole intention of the Messianic hope of Judaism. In 1869, and again in 1885, American Conferences of liberal Rabbis adopted resolutions to the following effect: 'The Messianic aim of Israel is not the restoration of the old Jewish State under a descendant of David, involving a second separation from the nations of the earth, but the union of all children of God in the confession of the unity of God, so as to realise the unity of all rational creatures and their call to moral sanctification.' This view sees in the destruction of the Temple and the dispersal of Israel not a punishment but a stage in the fulfilment of Israel's destiny as revealed to Abraham. Israel is High-Priest, and can only fulfil his mission in the close neighbourhood of those to whom he is elected to minister.

This, no less than the non-Messianic Zionism, is a considerable change from older beliefs. As a Messianic hope it transcends the visions of Isaiah. The prophet looks forward to an ideal future, a reign of peace and felicity, but the nations are to flow to Zion. The significance of the change lies in this. The Messianic idea now means to many Jews a belief in human development and progress, with the Jews filling the role of the Messianic people, but only as primus inter pares. It is the expression of a genuine optimism. 'Character, no less than Career,' said George Eliot, 'is a process and an unfolding.' So with the Character of mankind as a whole. But this idea of development, unfolding, is quite modern in the real sense of the terms; it is something outside the range even of the second Isaiah. Judaism was never quite sure whether to join the ranks of the 'laudatores temporis acti,' or to believe that man never is but always to be blest. On the one hand, the person of Adam was endowed with perfections such as none of his successors matched. On the other hand, the Golden Age of Judaism, as Kenan said, was thrown forward into the future. That on the whole Judaism has taken the prospective rather than the retrospective view, is the sole justification for the modern conception of the Messianic Age which is fast becoming predominant in the Synagogue. The Synagogue does not share the Roman poet's sentiment:

'A race of men baser than their sires
Gave birth to us, a progeny more vile,
Who dower the world with offspring viler still';
but the English poet's trust:

'Yet I doubt not through the ages one increasing purpose runs,
And the thoughts of men are widened with the process of the suns.'
Denouncing the 'Calculators of the End,' a Rabbi said (Sanh. 97 b): 'All the computed terms have passed, and the matter dependeth now on repentance and good deeds' (cf. S. Singer, The Messianic Idea in Judaism, pp. 1 and 18)

If, however, Israel is not destined to a Restoration, if the Jewish Mission is the propagation of an idea, on what ground is the continued existence of Israel as a separate organisation defensible or justified? Israel is indestructible, said Jehuda Halevi in the twelfth century; certainly Israel is undestroyed. When Frederick the Great asked what should make him believe in God, he received in answer, 'the survival of the Jews.' Dr. Guttmann of Breslau not long since put forward a similar plea in vindication of the continued significance of Judaism. In nature all forms die when their utility is over; in history, peoples succumb when their work in and for the world is complete. Shall, he asks, we recognise Judaism as the solitary exception, as the unique instance of the survival of the unfit and the unnecessary?

The modern apologists for all religions rarely belong to the rank and file. Whether it be Harnack for Christianity or Mr. Montefiore for Judaism, the vindicators stand far above the average of the believers whose faith they are vindicating. The average man needs no defence for a religion which enables him to live and thrive, materially and spiritually. The importance of this consideration is very great. Restricting our attention to Judaism, it is clear that it still offers ideals to many, prescribes and enforces a moral law, teaches a satisfying doctrine of God. If so, then it is futile to discuss whether Judaism is still necessary. Can the world afford to surrender a single one of its forces for good? If there are ten millions of men, women, and children who live, and live not ignobly, by Judaism, can it be contended that Judaism is obsolete? The first, the main justification of Judaism is its continued efficiency, its proved power still to control and inspire many millions of human lives. There are more people living as Jews to-day, than there were at any previous moment in the world's history.

But, like many answers to questions, this reply does not satisfy those who raise the question. I refer exclusively to the doubters among the Jews themselves, for if Jews were themselves convinced of the justification of the Jewish separateness, the rest of the world would be convinced. Now, the Jews who ask this question are those who are not so completely given over to Judaism, that they are blind to the claims of other religions. To them the question is one not of absolute, but of comparative truth. Judaism may still be a power, but it may not be a desirable power. The further question therefore arises as to the mission of Israel in history to come as well as in history past. History seems contradicted by the claim made by Judaism. Jews are quick enough to see the weakness of the pretension made by certain sects of dogmatic Christianity that it is the last word of religion, that all saving truth was once for all revealed some nineteen centuries ago. History, says the Jewish controversialist, teaches no such lessons of finality. Forces appear, work their destined course, and then make way for other forces. The world does not stand still; it moves on. Then how can Judaism claim for itself a permanence, a finality, which it must deny to every other system, to every other influence which has in its turn moulded human destiny?

A favourite answer is: Judaism is the exception that proves the rule. It has been a permanent force in the world's history. It is argued that Jewish ideals have exercised recurrent influence at all important crises. Dr. Guttmann somewhat rhetorically makes this identical claim. He points to the birth of

Christianity, the rise of Islam, the mediaeval Scholasticism, the Italian Renaissance, the German Reformation, the English and American Puritanism, the modern humanitarian movement, as exemplifications of the continued power of Judaism to mould the minds and souls of men. There is a sense in which this claim is just. It is a valuable support to the Jew's allegiance to Judaism. But even if Dr. Guttmann's claim were granted, and it is considerably exaggerated, how does it help? We are all agreed as to the debt which the world owes to Greece. That debt is a great one. Is it obsolete? Surely not. Greece has again and again revived its ancient power to inspire men. The world would be a poor one to-day without all that Greek culture stands for. Greece did not give men enough to live by; Hebraism did that. But Greece made life more worth living. Hellenism is an ever-recurrent force in human civilisation. Yet no one argues that because Hellenism is still necessary, Hellenes are also necessary. Who contends that for carrying on Greek culture you need Greeks? On the contrary, it was the case of Greece that gave rise to the profound observation that just as a man must die to live, so peoples must die that men may live through them. Renan, who, among the moderns, gave fullest value to this truth, included Judaea with Greece in the generalisation. Certainly as a nation, whether temporarily or irrevocably, Judaea perished no less than Athens, that a new world might be born. And a new Jewish nation would no more be the old Judaea of Isaiah than the Athens of to-day is the Athens of Pericles, or the Rome of to-day the Rome of Augustus. History does not retrace its steps.

Athens fell, and with it the Athenians. Why then, when Judaea fell, did the Jews remain? Greek culture does not need Greeks to carry it on; why does Jewish culture need Jews? The first suggestion to be offered is this:—Israel is the protestant people. Every religious or moral innovator has also been a protestant. Socrates, Jesus, Luther; Isaiah, Maimonides, Spinoza; all of them, besides their contributions—very unequal contributions—to the positive store of truth, assumed also the negative attitude of protesters. They refused to go with the multitude, to acquiesce in current conventions. They were all unpopular and even anti-popular. The Jews as a community have fulfilled, and are fulfilling, this protestant function. They have been and are unpopular just because of their protestant function. They refuse to go with the multitude; they refuse to acquiesce. Geiger used this argument very forcibly, from the spiritual point of view, in the early part of the nineteenth century, and Anatole Leroy-Beaulieu (in his book Israel among the Nations) even more forcibly used it at the end of the same century, from the historical point of view. This ingenious French observer cites a suspicion that 'the sons of Jacob, as compared with the rest of the human race, represent a higher state of evolution' (p. 232). No modern Jew would make so preposterous a claim. But when the same writer sees in the Jew a different stage of evolution, then he is on the right tack. Here is a passage which deserves to be quoted again and again: 'I have little taste, I confess, for uniformity; I leave that to the Jacobins. My ideal of a nation is not a monolith, nor a bronze formed at a single casting. It is better that a people should be composed of diverse elements and of many races. If the Jew differs from us, so much the better; he is the more likely to bring a little variety into the flat monotony of our modern civilization'. And the same argument applies to religions. There is a permanent value to the world in Israel's determined, protestant attitude. The handful of protestants who, in Elijah's day, refused to bow to Baal and to kiss him, were the real saviours of their generation. And though the world to-day is in no need of such salvation, still the Jew remains the finest exemplification of the truth that God fulfills Himself in many ways, lest one good custom should corrupt the world.

Then again, Judaism seems destined to survive because it represents at once the God-idea and the ethical idea. The liberal Jew, as well as the orthodox, believes that no other religion does this in the same way as does Judaism. Putting it crudely, the Jew would perhaps admit that Christianity has absorbed, developed, enlarged and purified the Hebrew ethics, but he would, rightly or wrongly, think that it has obscured by dogmatic accretions the Jewish Monotheism. On the other hand, the Jew would admit that Islam has absorbed and purified the Jewish Monotheism, but has done less of the flattery of imitation to the Hebrew ethics. Islam has certainly a pure creed; it freed itself from the entanglements of anthropomorphic metaphors and conceptions of God, which are apparent in the early strata of the Hebrew Bible, and from which Judaism, because of its reverence for the Bible, has not emancipated itself yet. But that it can emancipate itself is becoming progressively more clear. And even if we drop comparisons, Judaism stands for a life in which goodness and God are the paramount interests.

But, beyond all, the Jew believes himself to be a Witness to God. He thinks that on him, in some real sense, depends the fulfillment of the purposes of God. It may be an arrogant thought, but unlike most boasts it at once humiliates and ennobles, humiliates by the consciousness of what is, ennobles by the vision of what might be. After enumerating certain ethical and religious ideas which, he holds, Judaism still has to teach the world, the Rev. M. Joseph adds: 'But to the Jew himself, first of all, these truths are uttered. He is to help to win the world for the highest ideals. But if he is to succeed, he must himself be conspicuously faithful to them. He is the chosen, but his very election binds him to vigorous service of truth and righteousness. "Be ye clean, ye that bear the vessels of the Lord." Only when Israel proves by the nobility of his life that he deserves his holy vocation will the accomplishment of his mission be at hand. When all the peoples of the earth shall see that he is worthily called by the name of the Lord, the Divine name and law will be near to the attainment of their destined empire over the hearts of men' (Judaism as Creed and Life.

A community that believes it to fill this place in the Divine purpose deserves to live. Its separate existence is a means, not an end; for when all has been said, the one God carries with it the idea of one humanity. The Fatherhood of God implies the brotherhood of man. And so, amid all its trust that the long travail of centuries cannot fulfill itself in Israel's annihilation, amid all its particularism, there soars aloft the belief in the day when there will be no religions, but only Religion, when Israel will come together with other communions, or they with Israel. And so, thrice daily, in most Synagogues of Israel, this prayer is uttered: 'We therefore hope in Thee, O Lord our God, that we may speedily behold the glory of Thy might, when Thou wilt remove the abominations from the earth, and the idols will be utterly cut off; when the world will be perfected under the kingdom of the Almighty, and all the children of flesh will call upon Thy name, when Thou wilt turn unto Thee all the wicked of the earth. Let all the inhabitants of the world perceive and know that unto Thee every knee must bow, every tongue must swear. Before Thee, O Lord our God, let them bow and fall; and unto Thy glorious name let them give honors. Let them all accept the yoke of Thy kingdom, and do Thou reign over them speedily, and for ever and ever. For the Kingdom is Thine, and to all eternity Thou wilt reign in glory; as it is written in Thy Law, The Lord shall reign for ever and ever. And it is said, And the Lord shall be King over all the earth; in that day shall the Lord be One, and His name One.'

Modern Judaism, in short, claims no finality but what is expressed in that hope. It holds itself ready to develop, to modify, to absorb, to assimilate, except in so far as such processes seem inconsistent with this hope. Modern Jews think that in some respects the Rabbinic Judaism was an advance on the Biblical; they think further that their own modern Judaism is an advance on the Rabbinic. Judaism, as they conceive it, is the one religion, with a great history behind it, that does not claim the religious doctrines of some particular moment in its history to be the last word on Religion. It thinks that the last word is yet to be spoken, and is inspired with the confidence that its own continuance will make that last word fuller and truer when it comes, if it ever does come.